West of Everywhere

West
of
Everywhere

Larry Christianson

NORTH STAR PRESS OF ST. CLOUD, INC.

St. Cloud, Minnesota

Dedicated to Norma Christianson – who faces changes and challenges in life with courage and compassion. Keep on traveling into open horizons west of everywhere.

Cover art by Tom Plihal
Author photo by Norma Christianson

Copyright © 2010 Larry Christianson

ISBN-10: 0-87839-408-7
ISBN-13: 978-0-87839-408-1

Printed in the United States of America

First Edition: September 1, 2010

Published by
North Star Press of St. Cloud, Inc.
P.O. Box 451
St. Cloud, Minnesota 56302

northstarpress.com

info@northstarpress.com

LIST OF ILLUSTRATIONS

Table of Contents

HEARTS WEAVING

WEST OF EVERYWHERE

WEST OF EVERYWHERE

Still
Small voice
    of adoration,
    of adventure.

West of everywhere –
A vision expansive:
    open horizons,
    vast vistas,
    limitations stretching
        beyond stars.
Bright.
Bold and inviting.

West of everywhere –
Dreams weaving
    through joyful faces
        of heart.
And fabrics of humanity
    exotic,
    intriguing,
    inspiring.

Soaring spirits
    on winds of freedom
        and change.

September 2009 while camping solo at Sawbill Lake in the Boundary Waters

Out West

Horizons

OUT WEST HORIZONS

Out West horizons –
Rolling along through the years
   gathered into colorful patterns
   far away and near to heart.
Places and spaces.
Beneath and beyond
   compass point – W.
Pointing toward old journeys
   and new visions,
   and deep longings of the spirit.

Out West –
A well worn image
   expanding compass headings
     and map boundaries.
A wide open place
   dwelling within minds
     and inspiring hearts.
A vast space as varied
   as the imagination
     of humanity.

Out West –
   a welcomed retreat
   of vague definition
     or precise location.
For meaningful memories
   along open horizons
     of adventure.
For changing reflections
   on life fleeting
     and precious.
Beyond and beneath
   horizons in all directions
     west.

November 2009 as a companion to "Up North Reflections" and "Down South Deflections"

ALL ZEROS

All zeroes
    rolling across the meter.
Numerical witness
    to endurance
        and quality.

Many miles.
Lots of stories
    from fleeting times
        and intriguing places.

Flashback faces
    smile into a future
        of promises.
And more adventures
    still unknown,
    yet taking shape
        in dreams.

All zeroes –
    hope for sunshine days
    ahead.

August 1990 rolling the odometer past 100,000 on old Ford wagon

A Prairie Sunset

A silent solitude
     prevails,
     persists in gloomy
          moodiness.

Sweeping gently
     across the burnt-red
          plain.
Falling slowly
     from the big sky
     in those few
          precious moments.
When the sun
     takes welcome leave
          of the earth.

A prairie sunset
     hanging on the horizon,
     promising the earth relief
          from the blistering heat
          of day.

July 1975 out in Montana somewhere on US 2

RAIN STORIES

Rain stories
  splash through puddles
    of memory.
Soggy with time
  passing,
  erasing rough edges
    like swift currents
    smoothing stones.

In streams of life.
Healing streams
  flood through minds
    and hurting hearts
    as Red River rises.
As water flows
  and rough edges
    are made smooth.
And people who care
  tell stories.

In gathering gloom.
In penetrating shades
  of gray breaking
    through dawn showers.
Dripping.
Clinging in icy
  patterns
  on hearts heavy
    with grief.

March 2009 reflections on the inevitable connection of water and Springtime

On the Coast Highway

Ribbon of dreams.
Pacific Coast Highway
     through Malibu
          from Topanga Canyon
          to Zuma Beach.
Golden sun
     illuminating bright sea
     relentlessly rolling from afar,
          surf crashing on rock
               and sand.

People along the way.
Legal Grind –
     coffee and counsel
          for the weary.
Velocity Café –
     caffeine jolt
          for the journey.

High test.
Peak performance.
Keep on dreaming
     of vineyards awaiting ahead
     along the Central Coast.
Stretching to horizons.
Blending into arid hillsides
     and gentle mountain peaks.

Grapes of plenty.
Wine for the world.

June 2004 while driving on route 101 north from Los Angeles

ALONE ON THE PIER

Strolling
Alone on the pier.
Santa Barbara Shellfish Company –
    calamari frita,
      oysters plump and juicy,
      shrimp tender and tasty,
        and Corona
        cold and clear.

Old pier on the Pacific.
Calm evening currents
    swirling within hearts
    and all around the scene.

Sun sinking.
Spirits renewing
    even in the absence
    of funny brownies
      at Inn at East Beach.

June 2004 in California along the way driving from Los Angeles to San Francisco

BEYOND BLEAKNESS

Foggy morning
    misty,
    murky,
    darkening daylight
        in storm clouds.

Gathering.
Waiting on Spring snow
    arriving,
    falling fast
        in a fury.

A cold Spring
    breaking out of winter
        deep freeze.
Icy grip
    letting go gradually,
        grudgingly.
On landscapes barren
    and longing
    for simple renewal
        beyond bleakness.

Unfolding.
Unrolling like a can
    of sardines –
        moist,
        slippery.
Glistening with promise
    and hope anew.

March 2009 with Spring on the horizon

HOLDING HANDS

Hearts mingling.
In gratitude and grief
    holding hands
        as friends.

Companions.
On a trusted journey
    of compassion
        and comfort.
And love enduring
    in spirit perking,
    in new found
        appreciation,
        affirmation.

Humanity shared
    and graces discovered
        in humor,
        in laughter.

Renewing.

June 2009 reflections on humanity shared in special connections

DESERT RUN

A whole lot of nothing
    out here –

Desert run.
Asphalt ribbon
    rolling through cactus country,
    ancient rock formations
        and sagebrush waving
        in the Western wind.
To weary travelers
    passing through canyon lands
    all the wounded way
        from Phoenix to LA.

Morning star
    rising in rear view vision
    of beautifully painted sky
        in subtle streaks
        purple and pink.

Colorado River
    unfolding in fields of green
        finally fertile
        along boundaries of hope.

Desert Center
    crumbling in massive decay,
    sinking slowly into sands
        of time standing still.

Indio
    rising in majestic date palms,
    reaching for sweet heights
        of heaven aloft,
        of paradise lost.

And found.

All along the mainline
    from Phoenix to LA.

Palm Springs.
Morongo.
San Bernardino.

City of angels and demons
    tangling in sunset glow.

Desert highway
    running through barren places
      of the soul,
      of gloom.
On nearer edges of renewal
    dancing in shadows
    from golden sunshine
      on fire.

March 2003 while rolling west on I-10 in a rented Dodge Neon at 85 mph

MOHAVE

Mohave –

A name simple and crisp,
    spelling danger,
        disaster.
Forsaken landscape
    of stubble sagebrush,
      shifting sand,
      relentless wind
        howling.

Restless spooky spirit
    whispering in high desert
      mirage,
      mystery.
In unsettled quiet
    rattling shaky nerves
    with heat scorching
      everything,
      everyone.
Shimmering along horizons
    drier than arid,
      stark,
      barren.

Lonely land.
Mohave!!

June 2004 while in southern California

Dawn Drama

Summer glory
in sunshine warmth
and fresh breezes.

Blowing gently
upon the earth.
Soothing sensibilities
and credibilities
yearning for healing
and new possibilities.

Morning story
in voices fresh
and lingering.
Longings
of bird song
and scurrying.
Creatures.

Awakening anew
to dawn drama.

July 2009 while enjoying the peacefulness of early morning

DAKOTA DREAM

Dakota morning –
    wispy,
    wide open
       sky.

Stretching beyond horizons
    bright,
    bubbling over
       with ever new
       possibilities.

Dakota dream –
    cloudy,
    clear blue
       horizon.

Expanding imaginations
    free,
    flowing through
       images promising
       and empowering.

April 2005 rolling out of Fargo on a glorious Spring morning

RUGGED RAINIER

Rugged Rainier
    rising in lush
        forested, mountain
            beauty.
And devastation.
Clear cut destruction
    amplified from a vista
    atop an old fire tower,
        betraying logging
            frenzy.
And greed.

Rugged Rainier.
Crisscrossing landscape
    in curling dirt roads
    along slopes and valleys,
        revealing ugliness
            and progress.
Run rampant
    by lumber jacks
    and robber barons
        of old.

Rugged Rainier
    overlooking snow capped
        wilderness splendor.
And defoliation.

November 2009 from long ago fire tower photo in Washington back in 1974 with logging devastation contrasting mountain beauty

SUMMER DREAMING

Summer dreaming
    in the cold heart
        of winter.

Hanging on tight.
Penetrating deeper
    into sunshine
        bright.

And boldly beautiful.
Like sun dogs
    surrounding frigid light
        of early morning.
Sky streaking
    with thin blankets
        of color.
In pale shades
    of pink and orange
        and purple dim.

Winter thaw
    arriving on southern
        breezes gentle.
A fleeting respite
    of warmth
    and running water
        trickling,
        flowing.

In icy ribbons
    only to freeze again.

January 2009 longing for warm season on far horizon

ESCAPE TOMORROW

Escape tomorrow
　　for north country
　　　　wilderness.

Away from work pressures
　　and home responsibilities:
　　　　unplugged,
　　　　untucked,
　　　　unfettered.
Fancy free.

Like a lone loon
　　calling softly,
　　　　sweetly.
Airborne
　　on early morning
　　　　breeze
　　　　with surprise
　　　　　　and clarity.

Lone loon
　　beckoning all paddlers
　　to open wilderness
　　　　horizons.

July 2009 on the way north to open wilderness horizons

LAKE THREE CHURCH REVISITED

Another Sunday morning
    vacation away.

Skipping church in glory
    at Lake Three Church –
        revisited.
Same natural music
    in the pines,
        and wilderness choir
           of singing loons
           enhancing prayers
                of hushed solitude.

Big Island Camp vistas
    of creation beauty
        and splendor.
Offering different vantage point
    from the perspective
        of another "pew" –
Hardly a mile paddle
    down lake
        from High Camp.

Sermons still sound
    in quiet voices
        of water.
Lapping on rocky
    shorelines
        soothing.

July 2009 from big island camp in reprise of summer before

Still

Waters

MANY WATERS

Many waters
    flow
    from tiny droplets
        splattering,
        gathering.
On rock outcroppings
    and in crevices
    deep with erosion.

Many waters
    flow
    in three directions
        scattering,
        running.
From Giants Range
    all along highlands
    of Laurentian Divide.

Many waters
    flow
    toward great waterways
        calmly,
        dramatically.

North – to Hudson Bay
East – to Atlantic Ocean.
South – to Gulf of Mexico.
Always flowing
    on many waters.

July 2008 reflections from Giants Range on the Laurentian Divide in northern Minnesota

Fjord Vistas

Gentle mists
    of falling snow
        showers.

Unveiling simple beauty
    and peacefulness
    previously concealed
        in fragile feelings.
Of hearts mending
    and spirits healing.

Ice floe
    in the wake
    of time passages.
Like currents swirling,
        flowing,
        moving onward.

Along fjord vistas
    twirling gently
    in a calm Springtime
        breeze.

December 2009 in late winter wonder

26

Expansive Avenues

Beyond understanding
>   in trenches of turmoil
>>   brewing,
>>   stewing.

Into anxiety simmering,
>   bubbling,
>>   overflowing with paranoia
>>   aplenty.

Beneath comprehension
>   in waves of confusion
>>   mounting,
>>   pounding.
On rocky shorelines
>   shifting,
>   eroding,
>   changing with clarity
>>   dawning.

Surface realities
>   beneath,
>   and beyond.
Exploring expansive avenues
>   of spirituality
>>   together.
Connected in bonds
>   of compassion
>>   and love.

May 2009 not sure of where or why

SPRING PEEKING

Pussy willows.

A subtle signal
    of Spring peeking
      from stark branches
        of winter fading.
In delicate buds
    white and fuzzy,
      and fragile.

A signature gift
    of hopeful hearts,
    of longing spirits.

Waiting for ice out.
Open water returning
    from winter long
      captivity.

Buried far beneath
    a comforting blanket
    of smothering quiet
    and calm.

Now released in motion
    and renewed energy,
    and beauty.

April 2009 in memory of my father-in-law Wes Mickelson

MIRACLE GROW

Spring beauty.

Hiding in barrenness
    barely escaping
        bitter winds.

And warming breezes
    hardly avoiding
        welcome hints.
Basking in sunshine
    delight.

Miracle grow –
    soil and seeds,
    rain and sunshine,
    sprouts and shoots,
        and blossoms.

And flowers
    finally.

April 2009 as natural renewal arrives in the north country

KICKING HORSE

Kicking Horse Valley –
Power crashing
    through Rocky Mountain
      grandeur.

Forest growing.
Rock magnitude,
    majestic.
Water flowing
    eroding landscape,
    bending time,
    transforming elemental
      reality.
Eternal movement
    beyond,
    and before
      history.

Captain Courage
    came to conquer,
    and was conquered
      by horse
      kicking.
Hector mania
    echoes through
    Kicking Horse Canyon –
      living into future
        lore.

Larry Christianson

Kicking Horse Grill –
Tastes from around
    the world.
Food colliding
    in golden combinations.
Modernity motions
    in relaxing summertime
      splendor.

July 2002 in western Canada near Kicking Horse Pass

GREASE GAS

Deep fried octane
        bubbling,
        boiling in cooking vats
                of fuel.

Awaiting a recycled
        glory all along
        the tortured way
                toward renewed utility.

A both/and deal.
Working mysteriously
        for french fries,
        henny penny chicken
                and auto engines.
Producing agrarian populism
        sparkling in new economies
                of unusual mixtures.

Enough to clog arteries.
Enough to power pickups.
Enough to challenge Exxon
        and McDonalds.

Transforming nutritional death
        into a vitality
                of new life.
And opportunities
        as renewable,
                sustainable energy.

Burning grease.
Not gasoline.

June 2006 riding shotgun out in North Dakota on the grease run into Fargo

Church Coffee

Headache perking
    in watered down,
        wasting away
            church coffee.

Drowning Norwegians
    in swirling seas
        of fogginess.
From coast to coast
    and nearly halfway
        round the world –

Drinking way too much
    church coffee
    in a numbing,
        new definition
            of bland.

On pathetic bland
    flavorless,
    bodyless,
    boldless headache
        in the making!!

July 2007 in commemoration of bad coffee

SAWBILL SUMAC

Sawbill sumac
        streaming in shades
            of red,
                pink.

And burnt orange.
On Sawtooth hillsides
        golden in autumn
            glory.

Brightening passages coming –
        inevitable,
        and barren
            with beauty.

Renewed.

Dead still.
Perfectly quiet –
        no loons wailing,
        no mosquitoes buzzing,
        no squirrels scampering,
        not even a whisper
            of a breeze.

As evening cools,
        and calms the spirit.

September 2009 enjoying Fall alone in the boundary waters

AUTUMN SERENITY

Autumn serenity
    up on Sawbill Lake.

Lone paddler
    on wilderness waters
        and portages,
    in a spirit calm
        and fragile.
Alone –
    yet not lonely.

Lonely heart
    down on Kelso River.

Winding through brokenness
    like willows,
        weeping,
    bending in breezes
        weary.

And wandering pathways
    littered with hope.

September 2009 out of Sawbill Trail in the boundary waters

OPEN WATER

Deep autumn
　　　at landscape arboretum
　　　　outing.

Awakening inactivity
　　　in branches bare
　　　　and stark.
In rustic beauty.

Awaiting winter quiet,
　　　still arriving,
　　　soothing and still –
　　　　peacefulness.

Open water
　　　on the lakes.
On the eve
　　　of December –
　　　　unusual,
　　　　unreal.

A canoe country
　　　unique opportunity
　　　not to be missed,
　　　　nor passed by.

If only in imagination
　　　and wild dreaming
　　　　of paddling.

November 2009 wondering what if . . .

36

SACRED VOICES

Sacred voices.

Whispering
    from deep within
    and far away
        in time and place.

Lingering
    on gentle mists
    yearning for clarity.
Emerging
    from foggy mornings
    into the bright,
        shining hope
        of a new day.

Swirling
    through healing hearts
        and lifting spirits.
Moving
    through present moments
    along the way
        from the past
        into future realities.

Speaking messages
    and meanings
        from deep within
        the center of mystery.

Sacred voices.

February 2007 while at an interfaith service in downtown Minneapolis

WILDERNESS DEVASTATION

Red Paddle bistro
    overlook,
    onto Canada north
        across Gunflint Lake.

Vista of wilderness
    devastation,
    in troubling wake
        of Ham Lake.

Forest fire.

Burned rock outcroppings
    stand stark
    and stripped bare
        of lichens.

Blackened forest background
    on new shoots
        greening,
        growing.

Into hopeful futures
    unfolding,
    unveiling
    beyond boundaries
        of time
        and place.

June 2009 from the bar at Gunflint Lodge

SAGANAGA SUSHI

Saganaga sushi
    with generous compliments
        to King Oscar.

At trails end.
At Seagull landing
    with gunflint gleaming
        golden.
In wilderness sunshine
    splendor,
    and wind whipped
        rain squalls.

A wonder to behold
    from angles personal
        and political.
Perspectives dangle
    in patterns illusive,
        reclusive.

In hiding hermits
    and starving artists.

June 2009 while picnicking on the Gunflint Trail

MILLBRAE WORD PLAY

Downtown Millbrae.

Hanging around
    in warm sunshine
    of a California
        late winter
        afternoon.

Word play
    at Peet's –
    tea and coffee,
        dark,
        robust,
    bursting with flavor.

Or Pete –
    old friend
    back in Wisconsin
        on the lake
        at Chetek.

March 2005 relaxing after a glorious flight into San Francisco

HUARAPI

Huarapi.

Thai house sauce
　　　with calamari
　　　and asparagus
　　　　　stir fried.
Gently.
Tender and spicy,
　　　crisply real
　　　on El Camino.

Singa.
Premium lager
　　　brewed in Bangkok
　　　by Boon Rawd
　　　　　since 1933.

Before Tojo
　　　and wartime disruption,
　　　turbulence and turmoil
　　　　　way before Nixon.

And dislocation.

May 2006 at Thai Stick in Millbrae, California

CATTAIL CAFE

Adapt ability
    surfacing in deep waters
       of change,
       and challenges.

Anew.
On trampled ground
    of roots tangling,
       twisting.

Growing again.
In friendship shining
    at Cattail Café
    nestled on sweeping lawn
       amphitheatre.
Burandt Lake
    wedding celebration
       of joy and love,
       of food and drink.

And upbeat music
    rocking the night
    by Traveled Ground
       friends.

July 2009 at a friend's outdoor wedding

COTTONWOOD SNOWSTORM

Cottonwood snowstorm
    fluttering gently
    on breezes light
       and fluffy.

Falling freely.
White as summer
    snow.
On sun soaked
    pathways
    at old Bay Beach.

Rustic amusement park
    along rugged shoreline
      Green Bay.

Bringing together
    generations of people –
      old and young.
In time collapsing
    in laps of fun.

June 2009 while at Bay Beach for a three generation family outing

Narcotic Horizons

Morphine mellow
    in a dope zone
    of rapidly diminishing
      clarity.

And disconnected perceptions
    floating through dreams:
      baking cookies,
      writing riddles,
      imagining healthy
        days.

Beyond narcotic horizons
    in brief interlude
      suspended between
      major surgeries.

A few short weeks
    perched precariously
    in the midst
      of weakness,
      of recovering strength.

And return to activity.

November 2009 from the hospital post-surgery

BACK FLUSHED

Back flushed –
      running upstream,
      flowing counter
          to gravity.

Across the grain
      of natural tendencies
          and sensitivities.

NG tube torture.

Twisting bowel
      in abdominal knot
      of intense pain
          and obstruction.

Untwisting blockage
      in surgical expertise
      of immediate relief
          and clearing.

October 2009 while enduring at the hospital

HEALING STRAINS

Narcotic fog.
Lifting slowly
    in fuzzy waves
        of uncertainty.

In shimmering fields
    of confusion.
Burning away
    in welcome glimmers
        of clarity.

In healing strains
    of gentle calm,
        compassion.
Flowing through streams
    littered with stones,
    stained by leaves
        rotting,
        decomposing.

In time passing –
    inevitably.

October 2009 while home recuperating from major surgery

SWEETGRASS

Sweetgrass.
Springtime in Montana
        mountain valleys
              and prairies.
Rolling beyond horizons
        of unseen promise
              and hope.

Sweetgrass.
Border crossing confusion
        at customs house
              Canada.
Answering simple questions
        with nothing to hide
        and only humor
              to share.

Though not welcomed.
While watching
        five Australians
        up against the wall
              being frisked.

For what could
        only be guessed –
        sweet grass,
              perhaps!!

April 2010 remembering a long ago border hassle from back in 1975

47

BLUEFIELDS LAGOON

Bluefields lagoon.
Waterfront activity
    bustling,
    bursting bonds
        of restraint.

And economic captivity
    gripping,
    grabbing fronds
        of hope.
In slivers of momentum
    waving on breezes
        warm,
        worthy.

Like palm trees
    on tropical coastlines
        of humanity.

And opportunities
    shrinking,
    sinking in diminishing
        spirits.

April 2009 for Oliver Hodgson and all Nicaraguan friends

CANTINA CULTURE

Cantina culture.

Vibrant colors
      twirling in kaleidoscope
          atmosphere,
    spinning in wild
        wonder.

Brimming.
Bursting.
Overflowing
     with salsa music
     and spicy comida
        and ice cold.

Cervesa.

March 2008 at Chaska My Love restaurant

BLUE WATER CAFE

Blue Water Café.

Meeting place
    in Grand Marais –
    like Brittons
        in Ely.

On the other side
    of boundary waters.
On the same side
    of basic breakfast food
        and hot coffee.
Blending
    with local characters
    and wilderness paddlers
        hanging together.
Along picturesque
    harbor beauty.

Lake Superior
    painted on mural wall,
    portrayed in photographs
        and framed majestically
        by large windows.

For real.

June 2009 while up north promoting books

GUNFLINT TAVERN

Money.

May not grow
    on trees.
But it hangs free –
    bills taped together
    behind the bar.

At Gunflint Tavern
    on the waterfront
    in Grand Marais.

International cash
    joining a diverse array
    of food and drinks,
        and memorabilia.

All the world round.

In a colorful testimony
    to cultural connections
        and geography.

Woven together
    in a north shore
        tapestry.

April 2009 hanging around in Grand Marais

BUTTERFLIES GLISTENING

Butterflies are free
and beautiful –
a simple delight,
a vital witness.

To changes.
To transformations
lurking within seeds
awaiting.

Nourishment
in loving sunshine
and hopeful droplets
glistening.

In visions.
In ventures
looming beyond needs
arising.

February 2009 reflecting on Spring on far horizons

PICNIC RAPIDS

Picnic rapids
    on wilderness point
        rocky outcropping,
        blueberry picking
            paradise.

In spite of Bob saying:
    "I'd rather go to prison
        than pick blueberries."

Tumbling waters
    whispering in voices
        quiet.

And serene.

Tumbling down
    rocky hillside hike.
Rolling fast.
Crashing fall
    on stiff shoulder
        and bruised hip.

Hurting spirit
    more than body.

August 2009 out in the wilderness at Lake Four

CARIBOU FALLS

Deep.
In highland forest –
    ancient boreal,
    towering stands of pine
      along hillsides
      and in ravines.
Claiming rugged terrain.
Leading onward,
    upward.

Toward the falls –
    locked in winter's
      icy grip.
Snow covered energy
    captured in wait,
    longing for a thawing
      release
      of spring's waters –
    trickling,
    tumbling over slicked smooth,
      glistening black stone
        ledge,
    dropping in cascades
      through narrow gorge.

Falling –
    stunning in beautiful
      splendor,
    shimmering rainbow colors
      along a thundering,

crashing.
Descent into Caribou River
waiting far below,
swollen
and raging.
Running free.
All the way
to Lake Superior.

June 2007 to accompany Norma's late winter photograph from the north shore

CAMP 18

Sunset highway
    at mile post 18
    old logging camp.

Lumberjack restaurant
    dwelling in museum
        atmosphere.

History on display.
In massive log beam
    construction.
Old growth Douglas Fir
    forest destruction.

And great food
    in gigantic proportions
    along ragged shores
        of Humbug Creek.

March 2003 on the way out to the Oregon coast

56

MELLOW VOICE

Way down the coast
    from Pacifica
    to Santa Cruz.

How much credibility
    left to gain
        or lose?

Mellow voice seeping
    from the radio –
        familiar,
        haunting,
        lonesome
strains.

Of Sugar Mountain.

Innocence long time gone,
    blending,
    fading into a new
        peacefulness.

Sunday morning.
Acoustic sunrise
    at Café Pacifica.

February 2002 bumming around early morning Pacifica, California

MAGIC NUMBER

Barry.
And the Babe.

Tangling along the bay
     across complex divides
     of time and place,
        and especially race.
On the final stop
     toward baseball's
     treasured magic number:
       714!!

Finally –
And still Hammerin' Hank
     remains the homer king
     as the drama
       keeps unfolding.

May 2006 while in San Francisco as Barry Bonds finally caught Babe Ruth

LOST LUSTER

Barry.
And the Hammer.

Mingling through the heartland
      across simple connections
      of race and place,
            and lost luster.
On another leg
      of baseball's
      tarnished magic number:
          755!!

Reluctantly –
And still A-Rod
      lurks in the shadows
      as a future
          homer king.

August 2007 a few weeks after Barry Bonds pounded past Henry Aaron

Classic Autumn

Classic Autumn.
Wind blowing cold
   through branches
     bare.

In leaves tumbling,
   crisp and brittle,
   along walkways
     glazed.

With first frost.
Glistening on fields
   golden with harvest
     stubble.

On mornings brightening,
   clear and beautiful
   along horizons
     darkening.

With early snow.
Falling furiously
   on ground warm
     and still green.

Clinging precariously
   on tree trunks
    and branches
    laden with leaves.

Of many colors.

October 2009 reflections on season changing

AUTUMN PASSING

Autumn passing
    away –
        yet never completely
            gone.

Not vanished.
Remnants remain
        along hillsides changing,
                in streams flowing,
                in forests teeming
                        with life
                        and death.

Leaves in decay,
        deterioration –
        yet promising renewal
                and rebirth.

Winter embracing.

April 2003 in celebration of the cycle of life

SHARED WATERS

Shared waters
 of Oslo fjord.

Over a century
 of years passing
 between dreams
  of leaving
  and arriving.

From old country
 to new homeland –
  grieving,
  hoping,
  trusting.

As feelings meander
 through connections
 deeper than memory.

And far beyond time
 and place.

July 2003 on a dinner cruise ship on the water of Oslo fjord

On Oslo Fjord

From Royken city scenes
    across farm fields
    to old Christiana –
        way back yonder
        in the 1860's.

From Oslo Fjord
    to northern Wisconsin.

From struggles unknown
    and hardships unnamed,
    lost in passing time
        and people.

Forgotten yet familiar
    in fragmentary landscapes
    of yearning hearts
        and hopeful spirits.

May 2007 with my great greatgrandpa Andreas Killingstadt in mind

SMOOTHING OUT

Not roughing it
    in wilderness places
        of solitude.

And challenge.
But smoothing out
    in ancient patterns
        of sunshine.
And moon.
And waters lapping
    on rocky shorelines
    in relaxing rhythms
        of calm.
And contentment.

Smoothing out
    rough edges
        of daily life –
Like water action
    through time passing
        relentlessly.
Rolling on stones
    scattered along beaches
    cluttered with debris
        accumulating.

In ragged patterns
    of wounded experiences
        mending,
        healing.
Smoothing out
    slowly.

February 2010 thinking about roughing it and smoothing rough edges of life

Hearts
Weaving

RUNS A RIVER

Through every heart
    runs a river –
    love rolling on,
        always onward.

Toward distant horizons
    unknown,
    yet mysteriously woven
        from shared patterns.

And possibilities.

Strands of meaning –
    meandering
    in currents flowing,
        always moving.

Toward streams of joy
    and togetherness
        growing.
Runs a river
    through your heart
        and mine.

July 2007 from solo canoe trip on Kawishiwi River, for Norma over on Lake One

Intertwined

Hurrying dawn
> from a dark chill
>> of night.

Embracing fragile hopes
> and lingering fears,
> mingling together
>> in lonely hearts.

Everywhere –
> in morning light
>> with our love.

Intertwined.

Woven through time
> and place,
> and sorrows
>> and joy.

And our hearts.
Always!!

November 2009 in the midst of illness and uncertainty

GRANITE GROWING

Ancient boulder
    nestled deep
    in forest gloom.
Brooding among cedars
    and decaying deadfall
        uprooted.
Strewn haphazardly.
Scattered across forest floor
    emerging with new life
    growing from dying,
        old realities.

Ancient boulder
    cradled gently
    in glacial loom.
Sprouting lush carpets
    of moss and lichens,
        and ferns.
Amazingly huge ferns –
    delicate,
    deep green,
    delightful surprise
        atop "Fern Rock."

As big as my car.
In full biffy view
    on a relaxing
        autumn morning.

September 2009 from large boulder by the biffy while camping on Sawbill Lake

GOOD WEARY

Weary.
In a very good
    way.
Healthy aches
    and pains.

Paddling along wilderness
    waterways
      to ancient rhythms.
Beyond time.

And without regard
    to calendars
    and clocks
      and schedules.

Causing weariness
    in worldly
      ways.

July 2008 relaxing at camp after a paddling day in the boundary waters

70

CATALOGUE CAMPERS

Catalogue campers
    marching out of pages
        slick,
        sleek,
        stylish.

L.L. Bean
    for the woods,
    for wilderness fashion
        not function.

Decked out
    in spiffy duds,
    in trendy threads.

Dandy outdoor gear
    for indoors people,
    for chameleon campers
        driven by appearances.

And perceptions.
In L.L. Bean
    reality land.

October 2009 just paying attention while playing around with words

DIMINISHING DISTINCTIONS

Distinctions vanish
    in the haze
        of aging,
        of years.

Passing away
    in certainty diminishing
    and clarity fading
        in a fog
        of acceptance.

Diminishing distinctions
    in letting go
        of answers,
        of questions.

Searching dimly
    in contented hearts
        of joy,
        of hope.

And compassion.

August 2009 reflections from working in a nursing home

Unearned Wisdom

Unearned wisdom
    in white hair
        long.

And flowing free.
Liberated from restraints
    and old constraints
        of a rigid.
Worldview.

Earned folly
    in careless actions
        gone.

And being bound.
Captured in constraints
    and new restraints
        of a flexible.
Memory.

Someday.
Hopefully blending
    into a real
        wisdom.
Tempered by time
    rolling along.

November 2008 connections between aging and white hair

BAPTISM TREES

Mt. Morris.
Landscape of growth
    and change –
        personal history,
        family connections.
Running deep
    and far back
        in time.

In renewal of life
    expressed in trees
    planted in honor,
        and name.

Baptism trees –
    for beloved brothers
    Wesley and Jack.

Red maple reflections
    for young grandsons.
Threads of meaning
    winding through hearts
        of love.
Strong in the face
    of stormy winds
        of life.

Uplifted branches
    and beautiful leaves
        of hope.

Larry Christianson

Reaching high
>   with outstretched arms
>   of comfort.

And gratitude.

August 2009 for grandsons Wesley and Jack – trees planted at Camp Mt. Morris in Wisconsin as baptism gifts from friends Esther and Ray Glas

Up High

Up high.

Aloft on gentle
      currents of love
          and joy.

And imagination.
Lofty dreams.
Fluffy sky.

Spirits soaring
      to new heights
      of exhileration
          and adventure.

Balloon rising,
      floating free
      over St. Croix –
          hopefully.

Up high.

July 2006 for grandson Wesley our "Up High" boy

JUMPING JACK

Jumping Jack
        joy –
        a loving boy.

On the move.
Bubbling with energy
        and enthusiasm.
Tracing lines of recognition
        through absence:
                "poppa coffee."

To be known
        by a nearly antique
Tigers coffee mug.
In olde English
        D – for Detroit.
        1984 World Series
                souvenir ceramic.
Commemorating
        the "bless you boys"
        championship season.

Jumping Jack
        joy –
        blessed now
                and always.

September 2007 for grandson Jack

Denim Grandma

Denim Grandma –
    gleam in bright eyes
        dancing with radiance,
        sparkling with love,
   ever new
   always bright
        through years gone by.

Radiant lady.
Denim queen.
Rugged beauty
   in the continuity parade
       of giving birth
       to a new generation
       now bringing forth.

New life into being,
   into this old world.

Lovely
   new grandma.

March 2004 – for Wesley and Norma, his first time grandma

OLD GRANDPA

Old Grandpa –
      rocking middle age
          away
    on the shaky porch
        of a new day.

New grandson
      so fine –
    on loan to enjoy
        in calm arms.

Dreams glide
      across open minds,
      through long waiting
        hearts.

Generations collide
      with time passing
        swiftly,
    and unite in love
        growing instantly.

Contented
    old grandpa.

March 2004 - for Wesley and me, his first time grandpa

WRITER'S BENCH

Weathered bench
    in big pines –
        simple,
        rustic.

Overlooking little creek
    meandering slowly
    through majestic forest –
        dark,
        deep.

And laden with mystery
    and memories
    fresh with feelings,
        old and new.

Alike.
Aplenty.
Alive with spirit
    tumbling through times
        with Dad.

Before and after
    writers bench.

August 2008 at Mt. Morris in Wisconsin while camping with family and thinking about connections between generations – especially Dad and the little boys Wesley and Jack

THE POET

Words –
Rise on fragile
      wings of imagination,
           of vision.
Seeing with senses
      beneath and beyond
           reality.

Metaphors –
Emerge from sudden
      winds of complexity,
           of simplicity.
Swirling with possibilities
      fuzzy and formed
           firmly.

Images –
Unfold with natural
      wonders of creation,
           of creativity.
Bursting with meanings
      known and unknown
           freely.

March 2006 self-reflection while driving mindlessly across Wisconsin

LONG SLUMBER

Homeward bound.
On familiar roads
    of the heart.
Charting a course
    through time
        passing swiftly.

And rolling along.
On unknown pathways
    of the spirit.
Long slumber
    coming in welcome
        relief.
From personal burdens
    and responsibilities
    beyond belief.

Rest in peace.
Slumber deeper
    than eternity.

May 2009 with death in mind

Near At Heart

Far away.
Near at heart.

A juxtaposition
    only understood
    among friends
        and lovers.

A paradox
    too confusing
    for the casual
        and crazy.

A connection
    binding together
    kindred spirits
        forever.

Near at heart.
Far away.

February 2007 reflections on close relationships

Sorrow Whispers

Whisper of sorrow
    sighing
    soundlessly
        on mellow breezes.

Blowing within hearts
    of sadness
        weeping
      silently.

In the melody
    of ancient runes
      rising,
        connecting quietly.

Beyond all words.
Beyond all time
    and timelessness.

May 2007 rising from somewhere sad deep within my heart

FLEETWOOD MAC

Fleetwood Mac.
Rumours of invasion
    second wave,
    british style.

In the sixties
    returning,
    revolving through aging
        realities.

Unleashed.
Listening through big
    wall of sound.
Like thunder crashing,
    booming,
    rocking,
    rolling through rhythms
        rising.

Hopelessly finding
    a long way back,
        or forward.

Without hopeful hearts
    and lifting spirits
    in shimmering reflections
        of getting older.

Through stormy times
    out into sunshine
        of love mesmerizing.

March 2009 from concert enjoyment in St. Paul

CHROME DREAMS

Dreams
Derailed
    in losses
    incomplete
        and complicated.

Bending through prisms
    of fuzzy light.
Shining through maizes
    of murky darkness.
Polishing chrome
    on tarnished dreams
    as life rolls
        along.

Chrome dreams –
    same old message
    as rust never sleeps:
        "It's better to burn out
            than fade away."

Prairie wind
    blowing,
    bringing meaning
        to life passages.

November 2007 while at Neil Young concert on campus at Northrop Auditorium in Minneapolis

DANCING QUEEN

Dancing Queen
    in whirling motion
    on a wild arc
        twirling
        through history.

Happening.
In modern music
    swirling in beats
    of electric vibrancy.

And personal vitality
    in sparkling eyes
        of intense joy.

Pulsating.
In dazzling rhythm
    and radiant beauty
    of the dancing queen.

August 2009 for Norma

First Day

Kindergarten boy
    on first day
        with passion.

For learning
    and experiencing anew
    simple wonders
        of the world.
For cherishing
    gifts of heart
        and life.

School days
    beginning again
    in open horizons
        bright.

And promising –
    full of growth
        and learning.
For children
    and teachers,
        too.

September 2009 for Wesley and Norma on the beginning of school

NOTABLE

Notes.
Playing on heartstrings
    of the spirit.

Love notes.
Floating on hopewings
    of peacefulness
        and serenity.
Gentle breezes
    flowing through melodies
        of joy.

Notable.
In being
    more than deeds.
In hearts and mind,
    and especially soul.

August 2008 playing around with words

FRESH BREEZE

Love.
Like a gentle
      wind –

Feel it blowing,
      moving,
      touching.

Caressing all that
      remains unseen,
      yet real.

Like a breeze –
      fresh,
      renewing,
      restoring.

Hope.

January 2008 for Norma

SHRINKING WORLD

Flu outbreak
    shrinks the world
        in a flash.

Faster than the speed
    of paranoia
        and fear.

Fueled by media
    frenzy,
        and internet hype
           striking.

H1N1 –
    a code word
        for panic.

Running rampant.
Spreading beyond
    borders of reason,
    and boundaries
        of sensibility.

April 2009 on the leading edge of an epidemic soon to fizzle

A Back Road Day

Winding ribbons
 of roadway
  laid out in patterns
   random.

Cutting through real
 countryside.
On gray highways
 off the mainline,
  leaving McCulture
   far behind.

Going nowhere
 and everywhere
 in the same breath
  of suspended time.

Lingering on horizons
 bright and clear –
  uncluttered,
  uncomplicated oasis.

In McWasteland.

August 2000 while rolling along off the freeway

SECOND SIXTIES

Dewey died.

Diminishing Springfield
    long defunct,
        yet always popular
            buffalo band.

Leaving only Richie
    and Stephen,
        and Neil.
Young no longer –
    yet still rockin'
        the world.

In a second sixties.

Rolling along
    with kindred spirits
        Barry.
And Neil Young.

Listening for breezes
    fresh,
    vibrant,
    liberating,
        real.

And more real.

February 2009 upon the death of former Buffalo Springfield guitarist Dewey Martin in LA

BRIDGE

Bridge.
Benefit concert
      at Shoreline Amphitheater
      on San Francisco Bay.

Communication connection
      for the children –
          disabled,
            differently abled.
School of wonder.
Celebration of learning
      in bits and bytes,
      in sounds and sights.

All acoustic –
      most of the time,
          anyway.
A mellow Neil opens
      in misty, fading daylight:
          "Sugar Mountain"
          "Do I Have to Come Right
               Out and Say It"
          "Field of Opportunity"

And the music rolls on
      and rocks through evening rain:
          Tegan and Sara
          Eddie Vedder
          Los Lonely Boys
          Sonic Youth
          Ben Harper and the Innocent Criminals
          Red Hot Chili Peppers

Tony Bennett –
Crooning for children everywhere,
     calling for the end
     of killing one another
          as human beings.

Past midnight.
Past rain into dim moonlight.

Neil Young returns ruggedly
     in melancholy intensity:
          "Pocahontas"
          "Harvest Moon"
          "Journey Through the Past"
          "On the Way Home"
          "Human Highway"
          "Old King"
          "Comes A Time"
          "Four Strong Winds"

Joined by Paul McCartney
     and new beatle band
     for a "long and winding"
          closing gala celebration.

Ending jam
     on a crowded stage
     featuring the whole cast,
          and the children.

A raucous new beginning:
     "Hey Jude"

October 2004 with Emily at Bridge Benefit Concert outdoors in San Francisco Bay area

Balm For What

Balm.
Lying in wait –
      hidden within seeds
        of suffering.

Like promises struggling
      to break free
        of restrictions,
        of limitations,
        of tiny visions.

Like hopes leaping
      to larger life
        in creations.
Beautiful.
And bold.

Balm.
Lying in wait –
      found among fragments
        of healing
        experienced.
And expressed in moments
      fleeting
        and fragile.

March 2009 with Spring in mind

OUTSKIRTS

On outskirts
    lurking around shadow
        edges.

In thorny hedges
    of uncertainty,
    of mystery unfolding
        along ledges.

Slippery with confusion
    and contentment.
Like porch dust
    swept away,
    clearing lingering cobwebs
        of winter.

Weariness.
Bringing new beginnings
    out of old sorrows
        and heartaches.

Renewing on outskirts
    of hope.

April 2009 in the transition of seasons of the heart

DRIZZLY DAY

Drizzly day
    in complex layers
        of gray.

Rolling on winds
    shifting,
    swirling –
        gusting,
        gathering.

Despondency.

Dive bomber
    osprey on wing –
        soaring,
        searching,
        spiraling,
        splashing.

Head long
    into Lake Three
        fishing.

August 2009 while paddling in the boundary waters

AUTUMN ADVENTURE

Autumn adventure
    in mid summer
        time frame.
Out of focus.

Early morning fuel up
    at Brittons Café.
And on the water
    at a chilly 46 degrees
    at Lake One landing.

On the freeway
    with too many
        paddlers.

And hapless portagers
    struggling to haul
    comforts of home
        into the wilderness.

July 2009 on summer canoe trip in the boundary waters

SOCKED IN

Socked in –

Grayness enveloping sky
    hardly moving,
      slipping slowly by
        without definition.

In renditions of shrouded
    thickness.
In waves of showers
    and mist falling
      softly,
      quietly.

At big island
    camp.

July 2009 with Norma camping on Lake Three big island site

Never Ending Autumn

Never ending Autumn.

Warmth lingers
    on the land
        waiting for winter,
    on winds of change
        and new challenges.

Golden leaves shimmer
    in afternoon sunshine,
    in light sinking low
        on the November horizon,
        bending in new patterns
          of meaning.

Geese flying from Canada
    late on flapping wings
        of south migration.

Is it an upper midwestern
    dream –
    or a global warming
        nightmare?

November 2005 with glorious weather continuing well beyond the Minnesota norm for Autumn

Hoping Helplessly

Surgery scene
    underway in a collision
        of relief.

And regret.
Back to the hospital
    reluctantly,
    inevitably,
    helplessly
        hoping.

Or hoping helplessly
    out of control –
        completely,
        totally.

With no doubt
    nor denial.
As the gurney
    rolls away
    to the operating room.

Saying "farewell" –
    while thinking
    "see you later"
        on the other side.

November 2009 while at Methodist Hospital for aneurysm surgery

Nursing Heart

Turning leaf
    in Autumn swirl
    of intense glory
        and splendor.

Flowing.
Unturning
    in natural process
    of gradual change
        and beauty.

Twirling compassion
    in nursing heart
    of gentle care
        and comfort.

Suffering.
Untwirling
    in bedside manner
    of sensitive compassion
        and caring.

October 2009 for the nurses at Waconia Ridgeview Medical Center

STONES ALONG THE WAY

Stones
>at Brussels Hill –
>flat and rugged.

Emerging
>from dirt rich
>>and ancient,
>>old and new alike,

>>rising relentlessly
>>>through earth layers
>>>looming in mystery.

Converging
>from streams of memory,
>>fresh and fuzzy,
>connections churning
>>through spectrums
>>of meaning.

Stones
>at Timmer Huset –
>on the walkways
>>of home
>>and heart.

Transported
>from farm and field,
>>lakeshore and hillside,
>scattered places near and far,
>gathered together

in rustic patterns
of faded glory.
Enduring
well beyond time
and place.

Stones along the way.

April 2004 from stone picking escapades

QUIET CORNERS

Quiet corners
of a healing heart
longing for calm
and comfort.

In an oasis
called home.

Solitude yearning
in soft voices
of compassion.

November 2009 on calming down and healing at home

ENDING YEAR

Ending year
> of political promise
>> and personal pain.

Rising hope
> in sunshine dim
>> and lingering long
>> through tattered fabrics.

Alive with colorful patterns
> dancing with beauty
> in ordinary troubles
>> on bumpy pathways.

Of year ending
> on upbeat strains
>> of health restoring.
And hope rising
> through sunshine bright
> and radiating calmly
>> through wounded hearts.

Awakening
> to new possibilities
>> shimmering with joy.

December 2009 for a tough year ending finally

West

of

Everywhere

TRACES OF THE HEART

West of longing –

A restless freedom
      engaging emotional reality
         in visions
         of mystery
            and wonder.

East of nowhere –

A new contentment
      following traces of the heart
         in journeys
         of unknown
            exploration.

September 2009 with hints of another book of poetry coming

SKY FARMS

Stretching
      through stark desert
        valleys –

Beyond smoggy horizons.
Teeming
      with unseen possibilities
      blowing in the wind.

Twirling
      through majestic arcs
        powerfully –

Beneath gleaming propellers.
Churning
      with natural motion
      farming in the sky.

March 2003 in the desert in southern California out near Palm Springs

ONLY STORIES

Only stories.
Outlast ongoing searches
    for easy answers
        to tough questions.

Too numerous
    to really matter,
    to make a difference.

Only stories.
Remain from wreckages
    of time
        rolling along.

Too rapidly
    to really notice,
    to capture more
        than fragments.

Only stories
    carry inspirational
        meaning.

October 2009 from who knows where

HISTORY DAY

In North Beach
>with the Beats,
>>slipping away slowly
>>>in shadows,
>>>>dim and distant
>>>>>from way too many
>>>>>daytime dreams.

City Lights Bookstore.
Birthplace
>of howling poetry
>>and Ike era rebellion
>>>on slippery edges
>>>>of beatnik beginnings.

Washington Square Park
Another urban patch
>of green space
>>named in honor
>>of old George.

Hardly a bohemian.
Not even resurrected
>in bronze grandeur
>by twisted views
>>of revisionists,
>>or pigeons flocking.
Far removed by time,
>yet always near
>as colonial sage

outlasting the Beats
and leftover hippies
on the wane.

Everywhere but the Haight.
Only a short trip
back to the summer
of love –
turning ugly
all too quickly.
Luster lost in a Gap
occupying the strategic corner
of Ashbury.

A vibrant energy
pulsating,
radiating hopefulness
through youthful idealism
along tattered edges
of burnouts.

History swirls
through crowded streets
and long faded memories
bittersweet.

May 2006 on a full day bumming around San Francisco

Swift Current

Swift current
    in a slow,
        steady.
Retreat.

Relaxation on sun time
    with day turning
        to night –
And back again
    relentlessly.

In predictable passages
    from light to darkness.
In the ongoing march
    of time marked
        by pauses.

From too much activity,
    too much frantic
        motion.
In swift currents
    flowing
        and fragile.

July 2009 from the boundary waters, not Saskatchewan

QUIET WIND

Quiet wind
    bending through tunnels
      of sorrow,
      of sadness.

Seeping.
Soothing rough edges
    broken,
    spoken in rhythms
      beyond words.

Sweeping.
Smoothing wrinkled souls
    restless,
    caress in compassion
      beneath gentleness.

April 2009 after a long winter

PIER 39

Harbor breeze
   blowing softly.

Mellow chill
   flowing gently,
     swirling in autumn air
       enlightening.

Music floating
   through walkways
     crowded with people
       all along the wharf.

Pier 39.

Atmosphere vibrant.
Alive with soul
   and spunk.

All in clear view
   of Alcatraz,
     shrouded in evening sky
       darkening.

October 2003 in San Francisco

INDIO

Oh –
Indio!!

Date capital
  of California.
Culinary center
  of Minneapolis
    uptown.
Of all northern
  places –

For south of the border
  comfort food.

Meats and fish.
Chiles and spices
  from Mexico.
All washed down
  with dos equis
    amber.

Indio –
Oh!!

May 2008 in Minneapolis with friends

GASSING UP IN WATTS

Pacifico.
Darkness.

More than night
    on Wilmington Avenue –
        in Watts.

South Central.

Urban ghetto
    LA style.
All our differences
    don't really need
    to make a difference
        unless –

Unless we let them.

Running on empty.
Filling up in Watts –
    of all places!!

February 2005 on a lonely night on the way to LAX

THUNDER ROAD

Lightning mirage
    shimmers in sweltering sun
    on desolate desert road.

Deserted.
Abandoned by time
    passing along
    in the sacred name
        of progress.
Or destruction.

Disguised by merchants
    of money,
    and greedy charlatans
        on shaky paths
        of improvement.

Landscape suffers.
Culture languishes
    and transforms
        into a comic.
Sub-cultural tragedy
    along old route 66.

Thunder road.

June 2006 inspired by the movie "Cars"

A Slower Pace

Day before escaping
    to north shore
        refuge,
        haven,
        hideout.

Retreat into a slower
    pace and relaxing
        spirit
        of renewal.

At Cove Point.

Winter ice hiding,
    sparkling,
    glistening in morning
        sunshine.
Shoreline rocks
    jumbled,
    jagged in Superior
        Springtime.

Awaiting warmth.

April 2009 with Norma at Cove Point Lodge near Beaver Bay

Up Here

Up here –
    as opposed
    to down there,
        or over yonder.

A wilderness designation
        transcending boundaries
            of time
            and place.

A natural attitude
        transforming understandings
            of nature
            and beauty.

July 2009 reflections on being up north

Diamond Rock

Ancient forces
    giving voice
    to connections
        deeper than humanity.
And older than time
    standing still in silhouettes
        passing eternally.

Diamond rock –
A precious relic
    deposited by glacial
        movements of ice
        upon the earth,
    crafted by erosion
        of wind and water,
        of rain cleansing.

And sun shining.
In all seasons.
In all centuries
    decorated by moss
        and lichens growing,
        and birds dropping.

Diamond rock –
A familiar landmark
    guiding all who travel
        by canoe,
    standing guard majestically
        at the gateway
        to Lake Four.

July 2008 at the channel leading east from Lake Three to Lake Four in the Boundary Waters Canoe Area Wilderness

LIFE PASSES

Life passes
        swiftly through scenes
           patterned,
           multi-layered.

Patched together
        randomly from fragments
           of joy,
           of sorrow
                and love.

Life flashes
        slowly through memories
           imperfect,
           blended.

Imprinted together
        haphazardly on fabrics
           of hurt,
           of heart
                and spirit.

November 2009 between surgeries

SWEET LOVE

Lonely day.
Far away.

Carmel-by-the-Sea.

Pacific breezes –
      balmy longings
      stir feelings
           of sweet love.

Dreams of togetherness.

Hear my heart
      whisper expressions
           of devotion,
           of deep undying
                connections.

Sweet love.

July 2004 for Norma while listening to folk singer Kate Wolf

November Sunset

November sunset
    in blaze orange
        sinking slowly.

In bare branches
    out on far edges
        of west.
Wide open horizons
    of new opportunities
        and hopeful possibilities.

In thanks living
    with a joyful heart
        full of love.
And gratitude.

In simple treasures
    and basic blessings
        of life.

Passing swiftly.
Shared in relationships
    of meaning.

November 2009 for Norma and a quiet, calm holiday home from the hospital